I0016954

This book is indispensable for anyone seeking a profound understanding of artificial intelligence and securing their place in the future of work. From foundational concepts to practical applications and ethical challenges, "Leading with AI" serves as an essential guide that prepares readers to adapt and thrive in an increasingly automated world.

Covering automation, optimization, and innovation in products and services, the book provides a comprehensive exploration of how AI is reshaping industries. It underscores AI's critical role in enhancing decision-making and operational efficiency, crucial for staying relevant in one's field and avoiding job obsolescence.

With detailed examples and case studies on large language models and advanced agent systems, "Leading with AI" demonstrates not only how AI can drive business success but also addresses the ethical and legal challenges of its implementation. Understanding these aspects is vital for responsibly deploying AI solutions, mitigating biases, and respecting privacy.

Moreover, the book offers clear and effective strategies for integrating AI into various operational areas, ensuring readers can apply this knowledge practically and effectively within their organizations. Discussions on complex systems and digital humans provide new insights into the interactive future of AI and humans.

In summary, "Leading with AI" is a must-read repeatedly recommended for those who wish to not only comprehend artificial intelligence but also leverage it to secure and enhance employability in the digital age. It equips readers with the necessary tools to tackle emerging challenges and capitalize on the opportunities AI presents, making this book essential reading to stay ahead in the rapidly evolving job landscape

Table of Contents

Chapter 1: Introduction: The Era of Artificial Intelligence

The 21st century has witnessed an unprecedented rise in the development and application of artificial intelligence (AI). AI technologies are transforming industries, redefining work, and opening new avenues for economic growth. This book aims to explore the various facets of AI, its current state, and its future potential. By understanding AI, we can better harness its power to generate wealth and improve lives globally.

AI's capabilities range from automating repetitive tasks to providing deep insights through data analysis. The potential for economic growth is immense, with AI-driven solutions enhancing productivity, reducing costs, and creating new markets. As we delve into the topics of AI, we will also explore how businesses and individuals can leverage these technologies to generate significant income.

The Transformative Power of AI

Artificial Intelligence is not just a technological advancement; it represents a fundamental shift in how we approach problems, make decisions, and create value. AI's ability to process vast amounts of data, recognize patterns, and make predictions enables it to tackle complex tasks that were previously beyond human capability. This transformative power can be harnessed in numerous ways to generate significant economic wealth.

AI and Economic Growth

AI's impact on economic growth is profound. It enhances productivity by automating routine tasks, enabling workers to focus on more strategic activities. For example, AI can automate customer service through chatbots, manage inventory through predictive analytics, and optimize supply chains through real-time data analysis. These applications reduce costs and increase efficiency, leading to higher profitability.

Moreover, AI opens up new markets and business models. Companies can leverage AI to offer personalized products and services, create innovative solutions, and tap into previously inaccessible customer segments. For instance, AI-driven personalized marketing can boost sales by tailoring recommendations to individual preferences, while AI-powered financial services can provide tailored investment advice and risk management solutions.

Opportunities for Wealth Generation

The era of AI presents countless opportunities for individuals and businesses to generate wealth. Here are some key areas where AI can be leveraged for financial success:

Entrepreneurship and Startups: AI lowers the barriers to entry for new businesses. Entrepreneurs can use AI to develop innovative products, improve customer experiences, and streamline operations. AI-driven startups can disrupt traditional industries by offering smarter, more efficient solutions.

Investment and Trading: AI algorithms can analyze market trends, predict stock movements, and execute trades with high precision. Investors and traders can use AI to gain a competitive edge, reduce risks, and maximize returns. Algorithmic trading platforms and robo-advisors are examples of AI applications in the financial sector.

Automation and Productivity: Businesses can implement AI to automate repetitive tasks, such as data entry, payroll processing, and customer support. This automation leads to significant cost savings and allows employees to focus on higher-value tasks, thereby increasing overall productivity and profitability.

Data Monetization: Companies can monetize the vast amounts of data they collect by using AI to extract valuable insights. These insights can inform business strategies, improve product development, and enhance customer engagement. Additionally, businesses can sell anonymized data to other organizations seeking to leverage AI.

AI as a Service: Providing AI solutions as a service (AIaaS) is a growing market. Companies that develop AI tools and platforms can offer them to other businesses on a subscription or usage-based model. This approach allows companies of all sizes to access advanced AI capabilities without significant upfront investment.

Case Studies of AI-Driven Wealth Generation

To illustrate the potential of AI in generating wealth, let's look at a few real-world examples:

Amazon: Amazon uses AI extensively to enhance its operations and customer experience. AI algorithms power its recommendation system, which drives a significant portion of its sales. Additionally, Amazon uses AI for inventory management, logistics optimization, and even in its cashier-less Amazon Go stores.

Alphabet (Google): Google leverages AI in various ways, from improving search algorithms to developing autonomous vehicles through its subsidiary Waymo. AI-driven advertising solutions also contribute to Google's substantial revenue by targeting ads more effectively.

Netflix: Netflix uses AI to personalize content recommendations, which keeps users engaged and reduces churn. The company also employs AI for content creation and optimizing streaming quality, contributing to its market dominance in the entertainment industry.

Tesla: Tesla's use of AI in developing autonomous driving technology has positioned it at the forefront of the automotive industry. AI enables Tesla vehicles to navigate complex environments, enhancing safety and efficiency. This innovation has significantly increased Tesla's market value and brand reputation.

Preparing for the AI-Driven Future

As AI continues to evolve, its potential for generating economic wealth will only expand. To capitalize on this opportunity, individuals and businesses must stay informed about AI advancements and actively seek ways to integrate AI into their operations. Here are a few steps to prepare for the AI-driven future:

Education and Training: Invest in learning about AI technologies and their applications. This knowledge will be crucial for making informed decisions and staying competitive in the AI era.

Innovation and Adaptation: Be open to adopting new technologies and experimenting with AI solutions. Innovation and adaptability are key to thriving in a rapidly changing landscape.

Collaboration and Networking: Engage with AI experts, join industry groups, and participate in AI-related events. Building a strong network can provide valuable insights and opportunities for collaboration.

Ethical Considerations: Ensure that AI implementations are ethical and transparent. Addressing ethical concerns and maintaining trust with customers and stakeholders is essential for long-term success.

By embracing AI and its transformative potential, we can unlock new pathways to wealth and create a prosperous future. This book will guide you through the intricacies of AI, from understanding its basics to exploring advanced applications, helping you navigate the era of artificial intelligence and capitalize on its immense opportunities.

Chapter 2: Understanding the Basics of AI

Artificial Intelligence (AI) is a rapidly evolving field that encompasses a broad range of technologies and methodologies. To fully appreciate its transformative potential and economic implications, it's essential to understand the fundamental concepts of AI, including Machine Learning (ML), Deep Learning (DL), and Reinforcement Learning (RL). This chapter provides a comprehensive overview of these key components, their applications, and how they can be leveraged to generate significant economic value.

Concepts of AI, Machine Learning, Deep Learning, and Reinorcement Learning

Artificial Intelligence (AI) refers to the development of computer systems capable of performing tasks that typically require human intelligence. These tasks include problem-solving, pattern recognition, decision-making, and natural language understanding. AI is the overarching field that includes various subfields such as Machine Learning, Deep Learning, and Reinforcement Learning.

Machine Learning (ML) is a subset of AI that focuses on the development of algorithms that enable computers to learn from and make predictions based on data. ML models identify patterns and relationships within data, allowing them to improve their performance over time without being explicitly programmed. There are several types of ML:

1. **Supervised Learning:** The model is trained on a labeled dataset, meaning that each training example is paired with an output label. The goal is for the model to learn to map inputs to the correct outputs. Common applications include classification and regression tasks.

2. **Unsupervised Learning:** The model is trained on an unlabeled dataset and must identify patterns and relationships within the data without any guidance. Clustering and dimensionality reduction are common techniques in unsupervised learning.
3. **Semi-Supervised Learning:** Combines both labeled and unlabeled data to improve learning accuracy. It's particularly useful when acquiring a fully labeled dataset is costly or time-consuming.
4. **Reinforcement Learning (RL):** A type of ML where an agent learns to make decisions by performing actions in an environment to achieve maximum cumulative reward. RL is highly effective in scenarios where decision-making sequences are crucial, such as robotics, game playing, and autonomous driving.

Deep Learning (DL) is a subset of ML that uses neural networks with many layers (hence the term "deep") to model complex patterns in large datasets. DL has driven many recent advances in AI, particularly in areas requiring large-scale data analysis such as image and speech recognition. Key components of DL include:

1. **Neural Networks:** Modeled after the human brain, these networks consist of interconnected layers of nodes (neurons). Each connection has a weight that is adjusted during training to minimize error.
2. **Convolutional Neural Networks (CNNs):** Primarily used for image processing, CNNs apply convolutional layers to detect spatial hierarchies in data.
3. **Recurrent Neural Networks (RNNs):** Effective for sequential data, RNNs have connections that form directed cycles, allowing them to maintain information across time steps. Long Short-Term Memory (LSTM) networks are a popular type of RNN that can capture long-term dependencies.

Reinforcement Learning (RL) is an area of ML where an agent learns to make decisions by taking actions in an environment to maximize some notion of cumulative reward. Unlike supervised learning, RL does not require labeled input/output pairs and instead relies on the agent exploring and exploiting its environment. Key components of RL include:

1. **Agent:** The learner or decision-maker.
2. **Environment:** Everything the agent interacts with.
3. **Action:** All possible moves the agent can make.
4. **State:** A situation returned by the environment.
5. **Reward:** The feedback from the environment to assess the action's effectiveness.

Different Types and Branches of AI

AI can be categorized into different types based on its capabilities and scope:

Narrow AI (Weak AI): This type of AI is designed and trained for a specific task. Narrow AI systems are highly specialized and cannot perform tasks outside their training. Examples include virtual assistants like Siri and Alexa, which can perform a wide range of functions but are limited to the scope of their programming.

General AI (Strong AI): General AI refers to systems that possess generalized human cognitive abilities. When presented with an unfamiliar task, a strong AI system can find a solution without human intervention. Although still theoretical, General AI aims to perform any intellectual task that a human can do.

Superintelligent AI: This is a level of intelligence that surpasses human intelligence across all fields. Superintelligent AI remains speculative and is a subject of philosophical and ethical discussions, particularly concerning its potential impact on society.

Applications and Economic Implications

Understanding the basic concepts of AI and its subfields is crucial for leveraging these technologies to generate economic value. Here are some practical applications and their implications for wealth generation:

Automation and Efficiency: AI can automate repetitive and mundane tasks, significantly increasing efficiency and reducing labor costs. For instance, robotic process automation (RPA) can handle data entry, transaction processing, and customer service inquiries, freeing up human workers for more strategic tasks.

Predictive Analytics: ML models can analyze historical data to predict future trends. Businesses use predictive analytics for demand forecasting, inventory management, and marketing strategies. By anticipating customer needs and market shifts, companies can optimize their operations and increase profitability.

Personalization: AI enables personalized customer experiences by analyzing user data to understand preferences and behavior. E-commerce platforms use recommendation engines to suggest products, streaming services personalize content, and marketers tailor campaigns to individual users. Personalized experiences enhance customer satisfaction and drive sales.

Healthcare: AI applications in healthcare include diagnostic tools, treatment recommendations, and patient monitoring. AI can analyze medical images, predict disease outbreaks, and optimize treatment plans, improving patient outcomes and reducing costs. The healthcare industry can achieve significant savings and efficiencies by adopting AI technologies.

Financial Services: AI transforms financial services through fraud detection, credit scoring, algorithmic trading, and personalized banking. AI systems can detect unusual transaction patterns indicative of fraud, assess credit risk with greater accuracy, and execute trades based on real-time data analysis. These applications enhance security, optimize investments, and improve customer service.

Manufacturing: AI-powered predictive maintenance can foresee equipment failures before they occur, minimizing downtime and extending machinery life. AI-driven quality control systems can detect defects on production lines, ensuring higher product quality and reducing waste.

Transportation and Logistics: Autonomous vehicles and AI-driven logistics optimization can revolutionize transportation. Self-driving cars and trucks promise safer, more efficient transport, while AI algorithms optimize routing and delivery schedules to reduce costs and improve service reliability.

Generating Income with Basic AI Concepts

To capitalize on the economic opportunities presented by AI, individuals and businesses must understand how to apply these basic concepts effectively:

1. **Entrepreneurship and Startups:** AI lowers the barriers to entry for new businesses. Entrepreneurs can use AI to develop innovative products, improve customer experiences, and streamline operations. AI-driven startups can disrupt traditional industries by offering smarter, more efficient solutions. For example, an entrepreneur could create a startup offering AI-based marketing analytics tools that help businesses optimize their advertising spend and increase conversion rates.
2. **Investment and Trading:** AI algorithms can analyze market trends, predict stock movements, and execute trades with high precision. Investors and traders can use AI to gain a competitive edge, reduce risks, and maximize returns. Algorithmic trading platforms and robo-advisors are examples of AI applications in the financial sector. By leveraging AI, traders can make more informed decisions, leading to higher profits.
3. **Automation and Productivity:** Businesses can implement AI to automate repetitive tasks, such as data entry, payroll processing, and customer support. This automation leads to significant cost savings and allows employees to focus on higher-value tasks, thereby

increasing overall productivity and profitability. A company might deploy an AI-powered customer service chatbot to handle common inquiries, freeing human agents to address more complex issues and enhancing customer satisfaction.

4. **Data Monetization:** Companies can monetize the vast amounts of data they collect by using AI to extract valuable insights. These insights can inform business strategies, improve product development, and enhance customer engagement. Additionally, businesses can sell anonymized data to other organizations seeking to leverage AI. For instance, a retail company could use AI to analyze purchase data and sell insights about consumer trends to suppliers and manufacturers.

5. **AI as a Service (AIaaS):** Providing AI solutions as a service (AIaaS) is a growing market. Companies that develop AI tools and platforms can offer them to other businesses on a subscription or usage-based model. This approach allows companies of all sizes to access advanced AI capabilities without significant upfront investment. An example could be a cloud-based AI platform offering image recognition services for various industries, such as healthcare for diagnostic purposes or security for surveillance.

In summary, understanding the basics of AI, including Machine Learning, Deep Learning, and Reinforcement Learning, is fundamental for leveraging these technologies to create economic value. AI's ability to automate tasks, provide predictive insights, and personalize experiences offers numerous opportunities for wealth generation. By staying informed about AI advancements and strategically applying these technologies, individuals and businesses can thrive in the era of artificial intelligence.

Chapter 3: The Revolution of Large Language Models (LLMs)

Large Language Models (LLMs) have revolutionized the field of artificial intelligence (AI) by demonstrating unprecedented capabilities in understanding and generating human language. These models, powered by vast amounts of data and advanced neural network architectures, are transforming industries, enabling new applications, and creating significant economic opportunities. This chapter delves into what LLMs are, why they are revolutionary, their applications, and how they can be leveraged to generate substantial income.

What Are LLMs and Why They Are Revolutionary

Large Language Models are a type of AI that uses deep learning techniques to process and generate natural language. These models, such as OpenAI's GPT-3 and Google's BERT, are trained on enormous datasets comprising text from books, articles, websites, and other textual sources. The sheer scale of these datasets, combined with sophisticated algorithms, allows LLMs to understand context, infer meaning, and produce coherent and contextually relevant text.

Key Features of LLMs:

Scale: LLMs are trained on billions of parameters, enabling them to capture intricate patterns and nuances in human language.

Versatility: They can perform a wide range of language tasks, including text generation, translation, summarization, and question-answering.

Contextual Understanding: LLMs excel at understanding the context of a conversation or text, making their outputs highly relevant and accurate.

Transfer Learning: These models can be fine-tuned for specific tasks using smaller, task-specific datasets, enhancing their performance in specialized applications.

The revolution brought about by LLMs lies in their ability to automate and enhance numerous language-related tasks, which previously required significant human effort. This capability not only boosts productivity but also opens up new business opportunities.

Generating Income with LLMs

LLMs offer myriad opportunities for generating income across various industries. Here are some key ways businesses and individuals can capitalize on these technologies:

Content Creation:

Automated Writing: LLMs can generate high-quality content for blogs, articles, marketing materials, and social media posts.

Businesses can reduce costs associated with hiring writers and increase content production speed.

Content Personalization: By analyzing user data, LLMs can create personalized content that resonates with individual users, enhancing engagement and driving sales.

Customer Support:

Chatbots: AI-powered chatbots can handle customer inquiries 24/7, providing instant responses and freeing up human agents for more complex tasks. This reduces operational costs and improves customer satisfaction.

Virtual Assistants: Advanced virtual assistants can manage a wide range of tasks, from scheduling appointments to providing detailed product information, enhancing customer experience.

Language Translation Services:

Multilingual Support: LLMs can provide accurate and context-aware translations, enabling businesses to expand globally and cater to a diverse customer base. Offering translation services powered by LLMs can be a lucrative business model.

Market Research and Analysis:

Sentiment Analysis: LLMs can analyze social media posts, reviews, and other textual data to gauge public sentiment about products, brands, or events. This information is valuable for marketing strategies and product development.

Trend Analysis: Businesses can use LLMs to identify emerging trends by analyzing large volumes of text data from various sources, helping them stay ahead of the competition.

Educational Tools:

Tutoring Systems: AI-driven tutoring systems can provide personalized learning experiences, adapting to the individual needs of students. These systems can offer explanations, answer questions, and generate practice exercises.

Content Summarization: LLMs can summarize lengthy educational materials, making it easier for students to grasp complex subjects quickly.

Creative Industries:

Script and Story Writing: LLMs can assist in writing scripts for movies, TV shows, and video games, providing creative suggestions and generating dialogue.

Music and Art Generation: Beyond text, LLMs can be adapted to generate music lyrics, poetry, and even visual art, opening new avenues in the creative industries.

Foundational Models: Definition, Usage, and Training

Foundational models are large pre-trained models that form the basis for various AI applications. These models are trained on diverse and extensive datasets to develop a broad understanding of language. Once trained, they can be fine-tuned for specific tasks using smaller, specialized datasets.

Training Foundational Models:

Data Collection: The first step involves gathering vast amounts of textual data from various sources, ensuring diversity and comprehensiveness.

Pre-training: The model is trained on this extensive dataset to learn language patterns, grammar, and context. This phase requires significant computational resources and time.

Fine-tuning: After pre-training, the model is further trained on task-specific data to optimize its performance for particular applications, such as translation, sentiment analysis, or customer support.

Foundational models are highly valuable because they can be adapted to numerous tasks, reducing the need for developing separate models from scratch for each application. This adaptability makes them a cost-effective solution for businesses seeking to implement AI.

Importance of Datasets in Training Models

Datasets play a crucial role in the effectiveness of LLMs. The quality, diversity, and size of the datasets directly impact the model's performance. Here's why datasets are so important:

Quality: High-quality datasets with accurate and relevant information ensure that the model learns correct language patterns and context.

Diversity: Diverse datasets that include a variety of topics, genres, and styles help the model generalize better, making it more versatile.

Size: Larger datasets provide more examples for the model to learn from, enhancing its ability to understand and generate complex language structures.

Businesses and researchers must prioritize obtaining and curating high-quality datasets to train effective LLMs. Collaborations, partnerships, and investments in data acquisition are essential for developing robust AI models.

Fine-Tuning: When and How to Do It

Fine-tuning involves taking a pre-trained foundational model and further training it on a smaller, specific dataset tailored to a particular task. Fine-tuning is essential when:

Specificity: The model needs to perform a task that requires specialized knowledge or context not extensively covered in the pre-training phase.

Customization: The model must be adapted to align with specific business needs or domain requirements.

Steps for Fine-Tuning:

Dataset Preparation: Compile a task-specific dataset that accurately represents the domain and requirements of the application.

Model Training: Train the pre-trained model on this dataset, adjusting the model's parameters to optimize performance for the specific task.

Evaluation and Adjustment: Evaluate the fine-tuned model's performance using relevant metrics and make necessary adjustments to improve accuracy and efficiency.

Fine-tuning enhances the model's relevance and effectiveness for specific applications, ensuring that businesses can achieve their desired outcomes.

Evaluating and Selecting the Right Foundational Model for Different Contexts

Selecting the right foundational model depends on several factors:

Task Complexity: The nature and complexity of the task determine the level of sophistication required in the model. For simple tasks, a basic model may suffice, while complex tasks may require more advanced models.

Data Availability: The availability of relevant, high-quality datasets for fine-tuning is crucial. A model that can be effectively fine-tuned with the available data will yield better results.

Computational Resources: The computational resources required for training and deploying the model must be considered. High-performance models may demand significant computational power and infrastructure.

Budget Constraints: The cost associated with training and deploying the model should align with the business's budget. Balancing performance with cost-efficiency is essential.

Businesses must carefully evaluate these factors to select the most suitable foundational model for their specific needs, ensuring optimal performance and return on investment.

Future Directions and Innovations in LLMs

The field of LLMs is continually evolving, with ongoing research and innovations pushing the boundaries of what these models can achieve. Future directions include:

Increased Model Efficiency: Developing more efficient models that require fewer computational resources while maintaining or improving performance.

Multimodal Models: Integrating multiple types of data, such as text, images, and audio, to create models that can understand and generate multimodal content.

Real-Time Adaptation: Enhancing models' ability to adapt to new information and contexts in real-time, improving their relevance and accuracy in dynamic environments.

Ethical AI: Addressing ethical concerns, such as bias and fairness, to ensure that LLMs are used responsibly and inclusively.

As LLMs continue to advance, their potential to generate economic value will expand, offering even more opportunities for businesses and individuals to leverage AI for wealth creation.

Chapter 4: Exploring the Limits of LLMs: Prompting and Memory

Analysis of the Limitations of LLMs

Despite their capabilities, LLMs have limitations:

- Contextual Understanding: Struggling with very long context windows.
- Bias and Fairness: Reflecting biases present in the training data.
- Real-Time Updating: Difficulty in integrating new information in real-time.

Understanding these limitations is crucial for developing effective AI strategies and ensuring the models are used appropriately.

Strategies for Effective Prompting to Overcome Model Limitations

Effective prompting can mitigate some limitations by:

- Providing clear and concise instructions.
- Using contextually relevant and well-structured prompts.
- Iteratively refining prompts based on the model's responses.

These strategies can improve the performance of LLMs in generating accurate and relevant responses, thereby enhancing their utility in various applications.

Solving the Context Window Problem

Techniques to handle context window limitations include:

- Chunking: Breaking down large inputs into smaller, manageable chunks.
- Memory Mechanisms: Incorporating external memory systems to store and retrieve context as needed.

These techniques can help extend the usability of LLMs in more complex and lengthy tasks, further broadening their application scope.

Chapter 5: RAGs and Agents: Advanced AI Systems

Chapter 5: RAGs and Agents: Advanced AI Systems

In the ever-evolving landscape of artificial intelligence, Retrieval-Augmented Generation (RAG) and intelligent agents stand out as two of the most sophisticated systems pushing the boundaries of what AI can achieve. This chapter delves into the complexities of these advanced AI systems, their operational mechanisms, applications, and the transformative impact they hold for various industries.

Understanding Retrieval-Augmented Generation (RAG)

Retrieval-Augmented Generation combines the best of both retrieval-based and generative AI systems to enhance the decision-making and response accuracy of models. This approach leverages a vast database of information from which it retrieves relevant data to supplement the generative process, thus ensuring that the output is not only contextually aware but also rich in detail and precision.

How RAG Works:

Retrieval Phase: Initially, when a query is presented, the system sifts through a large corpus of data to find relevant information. This step is crucial as it determines the quality of information that will be used to generate responses.

Augmentation Phase: The retrieved information is then fed into a generative model that synthesizes the input with its pre-existing knowledge base to produce a coherent and contextually appropriate output.

Integration Phase: Finally, the system integrates the generated output to ensure that it aligns with the initial query, adjusting for fluency, accuracy, and relevancy.

The power of RAG lies in its ability to pull from specific data points within vast datasets, providing answers that are not only accurate but also deeply informed by existing factual content, making it invaluable for fields like medical research, legal advice, and technical support.

The Role and Functionality of Intelligent Agents

Intelligent agents are systems designed to perceive their environment and take actions that maximize their chance of successfully achieving their goals. These agents are characterized by their autonomy, adaptability, and capability to make decisions based on real-time data.

Types of Intelligent Agents:

Reactive Agents: These are the simplest form of agents that react to changes in their environment. They do not retain past experiences and operate solely on the present data.

Proactive Agents: Unlike reactive agents, proactive agents can take initiatives based on their goals. They are not only responsive but also capable of anticipating future states.

Hybrid Agents: These agents combine the features of both reactive and proactive agents. They can react to immediate changes and plan based on long-term goals.

Applications of Intelligent Agents:

E-commerce: Agents can personalize shopping experiences by recommending products based on user behavior and preferences.

Smart Homes: Agents control home environments, learning and adapting to homeowners' preferences for lighting, temperature, and security.

Autonomous Vehicles: Agents perceive road conditions and make real-time driving decisions to optimize safety and route efficiency.

Challenges and Limitations

While RAGs and agents are advanced AI systems with broad applications, they are not without their challenges and limitations.

For RAGs:

Data Quality and Relevance: The effectiveness of RAGs heavily relies on the quality and relevance of the data they access. Poor data quality can lead to incorrect or irrelevant outputs.

Integration Complexity: Ensuring that the retrieved information seamlessly integrates with generative models to produce coherent outputs can be technically challenging.

For Intelligent Agents:

Complex Decision-Making: Agents often struggle with complex decision-making that requires deep understanding or moral judgements.

Adaptability: While agents are designed to adapt, their ability to cope with unexpected changes or novel scenarios is still limited compared to human flexibility.

Strategies for Effective Deployment

To maximize the benefits of RAGs and intelligent agents, certain strategies can be employed:

Enhanced Data Management: For RAGs, ensuring access to high-quality, comprehensive, and regularly updated data repositories will improve the relevance and accuracy of outputs.

Continuous Learning and Adaptation: Agents should be equipped with learning algorithms that allow them to evolve based on new data and experiences, enhancing their decision-making over time.

Interdisciplinary Integration: Combining insights from cognitive sciences, engineering, and data analytics can lead to the development of more robust and versatile agents.

Future Prospects

The future of RAGs and intelligent agents looks promising with potential advancements such as:

Greater Cognitive Capabilities: Enhancing the cognitive abilities of agents to handle more complex tasks and make more nuanced decisions.

Cross-Domain Functionality: Expanding the functionality of RAGs across different domains, enabling them to handle a wider range of queries and tasks.

Ethical AI Development: Addressing ethical concerns in AI, particularly in how agents make decisions and the transparency of RAG-generated content.

As these advanced systems continue to develop, they will undoubtedly open new avenues for innovation and efficiency across various sectors, fundamentally transforming how businesses operate and deliver services. The integration of RAGs and intelligent agents into daily operations not only optimizes performance but also fosters a more data-driven, responsive approach to meeting both current and future challenges.

Chapter 6: Practical Applications: How to Use AI

Evaluating the Value Contribution of Various AI Tools in the Market

AI tools contribute value in several ways:

- Automation: Streamlining repetitive tasks to increase efficiency.
- Optimization: Enhancing decision-making processes through data analysis.
- Innovation: Enabling new products and services.

Generating Income with AI Tools

- Automated Services: Offer AI-driven services such as automated bookkeeping, data entry, and scheduling, reducing operational costs and increasing profits. These services can be marketed to small and medium-sized businesses.
- Predictive Maintenance: Implement AI for predictive maintenance in manufacturing, reducing downtime and saving costs. This can be offered as a service to manufacturing companies.
- Market Analysis: Use AI to analyze market trends and consumer behavior, providing valuable insights to businesses. Companies can offer market analysis reports and consulting services.

Identifying Costs Associated with Different AI Solutions

Costs to consider include:

- Development Costs: Initial investment in AI model development and training.
- Operational Costs: Ongoing maintenance and computational resources.
- Implementation Costs: Integrating AI solutions into existing systems.

Understanding these costs is crucial for evaluating the ROI of AI investments and planning budgets effectively.

Global Landscape of AI, Key Players, and Future Development Factors

Key players in the AI landscape include:

- Tech Giants: Companies like Google, Microsoft, and OpenAI leading in AI research and development.
- Startups: Innovating with niche applications and cutting-edge technologies.
- Academia: Contributing foundational research and pushing the boundaries of AI capabilities.

Future development factors involve:

- Advancements in AI Research: Continual improvement in algorithms and models.
- Data Availability: Access to high-quality, diverse datasets.
- Ethical Considerations: Addressing ethical and societal impacts.

Steps to Implement AI-Based Projects

Implementing AI projects involves:

- Identifying Use Cases: Determining areas where AI can add value.
- Gathering Data: Collecting and preparing relevant datasets.
- Developing Models: Training and fine-tuning AI models.
- Integrating Solutions: Embedding AI into existing workflows and systems.
- Monitoring and Maintenance: Regularly updating and refining AI models.

These steps ensure a systematic approach to AI implementation, maximizing the potential benefits and minimizing risks.

Chapter 6: Practical Applications: How to Use AI

The proliferation of artificial intelligence (AI) technologies has had a transformative impact on multiple sectors, ranging from healthcare and finance to education and manufacturing. This chapter explores the practical applications of AI tools, evaluates their value contributions in the market, and discusses how these tools are reshaping industries by enhancing productivity, decision-making, and innovation. Insights from various sources, including specialized AI blogs and major publications like BBC Mundo, help illustrate the broad-reaching implications of AI technologies.

Automation: Streamlining Repetitive Tasks

One of the primary advantages of AI in the workplace is its ability to automate repetitive and time-consuming tasks. Automation not only speeds up processes but also increases accuracy and frees up human employees to focus on more complex and strategic activities.

Case Study: Robotic Process Automation in Banking

In the banking sector, Robotic Process Automation (RPA) is used extensively to automate routine tasks such as data entry, compliance reporting, and customer query handling. For example, JPMorgan Chase's COIN platform uses machine learning to extract information from legal documents, a process that previously consumed 360,000 hours of work each year by lawyers and loan officers. The automation of these tasks has drastically reduced the possibility of human error and expedited service delivery, leading to higher customer satisfaction and significant cost savings.

Impact on Employment

While there are concerns about AI leading to job displacement, many industries have found that automation actually creates jobs by generating demand for higher-level positions that require oversight and management of AI systems. Moreover, employees are often retrained to take on these new roles, adding value to the company and providing career advancement opportunities.

Optimization: Enhancing Decision-Making Processes

AI's ability to process and analyze large amounts of data in real time enables more informed and effective decision-making. This capability is crucial in environments where speed and accuracy are paramount.

Example: Supply Chain Optimization

In the manufacturing industry, AI tools are used to optimize supply chains by predicting and managing inventory levels, forecasting demand, and identifying potential disruptions before they occur. AI-driven analytics platforms can integrate data from various sources, including weather forecasts, current events, and historical data, to optimize procurement and distribution schedules. This results in reduced overhead costs, minimized waste, and improved delivery times.

AI in Healthcare Decision-Making

Healthcare providers utilize AI to enhance diagnostic accuracy and personalize treatment plans. AI algorithms can analyze medical imaging faster than human radiologists, with studies suggesting that AI can detect diseases such as cancer with greater accuracy than traditional methods. Additionally, AI-driven predictive models help healthcare systems manage resources more efficiently by forecasting patient admissions and optimizing staff allocation.

Innovation: Enabling New Products and Services

AI is a key driver of innovation, opening up new possibilities for products and services that were previously unimaginable.

Innovation in Consumer Electronics

AI has revolutionized consumer electronics through the development of smart home devices. Products like Amazon Echo and Google Home use AI to learn from user interactions, allowing them to provide personalized experiences through voice recognition and machine learning. These devices continuously evolve their functionalities based on user behavior, preferences, and feedback.

AI in Autonomous Vehicles

Autonomous vehicles represent a significant leap forward in transportation, made possible by AI. Companies like Tesla and Waymo have developed vehicles that can navigate complex traffic situations with minimal human intervention. The integration of AI not only promises to reduce road accidents caused by human error but also aims to optimize traffic flow and reduce carbon emissions.

Ethical Considerations and Social Impact

The deployment of AI technologies must be managed carefully to address ethical considerations and mitigate potential negative social impacts.

Bias and Fairness

AI systems are only as unbiased as the data they are trained on. If the training data contains biases, the AI's decisions will reflect these biases. This issue is particularly critical in sectors like law enforcement and recruiting, where biased AI could lead to unfair treatment of individuals based on race, gender, or age. Continuous efforts are needed to develop AI systems that are fair and transparent, with mechanisms in place to detect and correct biases.

Privacy and Data Protection

As AI systems often require vast amounts of data to function effectively, they raise significant privacy concerns. It is crucial to ensure that data used by AI systems is handled securely and in compliance with global data protection regulations, such as GDPR in Europe and CCPA in California. Companies must be transparent about their data usage policies and provide users with control over their own information.

Impact on Social Dynamics

AI also affects social dynamics, influencing how people interact with each other and with technology. The rise of AI-driven social media algorithms, for example, has changed how information is consumed and shared, impacting everything from political elections to personal relationships. It is vital to understand these dynamics to ensure that AI technologies are used responsibly and contribute positively to society.

Conclusion

AI tools offer significant benefits by automating tasks, optimizing operations, and driving innovation across various sectors. However, the successful integration of AI into society requires more than just technical excellence; it also demands careful consideration of ethical issues, proactive management of social impacts, and ongoing engagement with stakeholders to ensure that AI serves the common good. As AI technologies continue to evolve, they will undoubtedly provide even more opportunities for improving efficiency, making informed decisions, and creating innovative products and services, all while posing new challenges that will need to be addressed thoughtfully and effectively.

Chapter 7: Complex Systems and Digital Humans

Understanding Complex Systems and Their Management

Complex systems are characterized by:

- Interconnected Components: Multiple interacting parts with dynamic relationships.
- Emergent Behavior: Outcomes that arise from interactions rather than individual components.

Managing these systems involves:

- Systems Thinking: Understanding the whole system and its interactions.
- Adaptive Strategies: Being flexible and responsive to changes.

Impact of AI on Complexity

AI can help manage complexity by:

- Predictive Analytics: Anticipating changes and trends.
- Optimization Algorithms: Finding efficient solutions in complex scenarios.
- Simulation Models: Testing different strategies in virtual environments.

Generating Income with AI in Complex Systems

- Supply Chain Optimization: Use AI to optimize supply chain operations, reducing costs and improving efficiency. This service can be offered to logistics and manufacturing companies.

- Financial Modeling: Implement AI for complex financial modeling and risk assessment, offering services to financial institutions. This can include portfolio optimization, fraud detection, and more.
- Urban Planning: Provide AI-driven solutions for urban planning and smart city development. These solutions can be marketed to government agencies and urban planners.

Role of AI in Managing Complex Systems

AI assists in:

- Data Analysis: Processing vast amounts of data to identify patterns.
- Decision Support: Providing insights and recommendations.
- Automation: Streamlining processes and reducing manual intervention.

Digital Humans as a Case Study

Digital humans are AI-powered virtual beings that can:

- Interact Naturally: Engage in conversations with human-like understanding.
- Personalize Experiences: Tailor interactions based on individual preferences.
- Provide Consistent Service: Available 24/7 without fatigue.

Digital humans can be used in customer service, virtual training, and entertainment, offering new revenue streams for businesses.

Chapter 8: The Future of AI: General AI and Beyond

Current Market Landscape and Future Trends in AI

The AI market is rapidly evolving with trends such as:

- Integration of AI in Everyday Life: From smart homes to autonomous vehicles.
- Advances in Natural Language Processing: Enhancing human-computer interactions.
- AI for Social Good: Applications in healthcare, education, and environmental conservation.

These trends highlight the growing importance of AI in various aspects of life and its potential for driving economic growth.

How AI Can Improve Various Departments and Sectors

AI can transform:

- Healthcare: Improving diagnostics, personalized medicine, and patient care. AI solutions can be developed and marketed to healthcare providers and pharmaceutical companies.
- Finance: Enhancing fraud detection, risk management, and customer service. Financial institutions can leverage AI to improve their operations and offer new services.
- Retail: Optimizing supply chains, inventory management, and customer experiences. Retailers can use AI to enhance their operations and offer personalized shopping experiences.

Speculations on the Advent of General AI

General AI, or AGI (Artificial General Intelligence), would:

- Possess Human-Like Intelligence: Capable of understanding, learning, and applying knowledge across a wide range of tasks.
- Adapt to New Situations: Quickly learn and adapt to new environments and challenges.
- Potential Impacts: Transform industries, create new economic opportunities, and pose significant ethical and societal questions.

The development of General AI could lead to unprecedented economic growth and innovation, but also requires careful consideration of ethical and societal implications.

Chapter 9: Ethical and Legal Challenges of AI

As artificial intelligence (AI) continues to integrate into various aspects of society, it raises significant ethical dilemmas and legal challenges that must be addressed to ensure its responsible deployment and integration. This chapter explores these issues in depth, examining how they impact the social and economic spheres and outlining the frameworks that can mitigate these concerns.

Ethical Dilemmas and Legal Challenges Posed by AI Development

Bias and Fairness: AI systems often reflect the biases present in their training data or design. This can lead to unfair outcomes, such as racial or gender bias in hiring practices or loan approvals. Ensuring AI systems are fair and unbiased is crucial, not only for ethical reasons but also to enhance public trust and acceptance. Efforts to create fair AI involve diverse data collection, transparency in algorithms, and continuous monitoring for biased outcomes.

Privacy Concerns: AI systems capable of processing vast amounts of personal data can pose significant privacy risks. Ensuring the privacy of individuals becomes paramount as these systems become more pervasive in areas like surveillance, personal assistants, and health monitoring. Organizations must comply with data protection regulations such as GDPR in Europe or CCPA in California, which aim to protect personal information and provide users with control over their data.

Accountability: Determining who is responsible for AI-driven decisions can be challenging, especially when these decisions result in adverse outcomes. Is it the developers, the users, or the AI itself? Establishing clear accountability frameworks is essential to address potential harms caused by AI decisions, ensuring that there are mechanisms for redress and correction.

Impact of AI on Social and Economic Spheres

Job Displacement: Automation through AI can lead to significant job displacement, as machines can perform many tasks more efficiently than humans. This displacement can affect sectors like manufacturing, customer service, and even professional jobs such as law and accounting. To mitigate these effects, governments and organizations can invest in retraining and education programs to help workers transition to new roles that AI technologies create.

Economic Inequality: There is a growing concern that AI could exacerbate economic inequality by disproportionately benefiting those who have access to these technologies. As AI continues to advance, the gap between the 'AI haves' and 'have-nots' could widen, both within and between countries. Addressing this issue may require targeted policies to ensure equitable access to AI technologies and the benefits they bring.

Social Dynamics: AI also influences social dynamics, changing how individuals interact, form relationships, and view privacy. For example, AI-driven social media algorithms can influence public opinion and political dynamics by determining what information people see. Understanding and managing these changes are vital for maintaining social cohesion and ensuring that AI technologies enhance rather than disrupt societal norms.

Frameworks for Addressing Ethical and Legal Issues

Regulatory Policies: Developing comprehensive AI laws and guidelines is crucial for governing the use of AI. These regulations should aim to protect individuals' rights while also promoting innovation. Governments and international bodies play a critical role in crafting these policies, which must be adaptable to the fast-paced evolution of AI technologies.

Ethical Frameworks: Establishing ethical guidelines for AI development and use can help developers and companies navigate the moral implications of their technologies. These frameworks often emphasize principles such as transparency, justice, and respect for user autonomy. Industry standards and best practices can support the ethical deployment of AI, promoting a culture of responsibility among stakeholders.

Stakeholder Engagement: Effective governance of AI requires the involvement of a broad range of stakeholders, including ethicists, lawyers, technologists, and representatives from affected communities. Collaborative approaches can ensure that diverse perspectives are considered in the development and deployment of AI systems, leading to more balanced and effective solutions.

By addressing these ethical and legal challenges, stakeholders can ensure that AI technologies are developed and deployed in a manner that respects human rights, promotes societal welfare, and mitigates potential harms. The frameworks discussed provide a pathway for managing the complex issues associated with AI, but they require continuous evaluation and adaptation as the technologies and their applications evolve. This proactive approach in governance will be essential for harnessing the benefits of AI while safeguarding against its risks, thereby ensuring that AI serves as a tool for enhancing human capabilities and improving lives across the globe.

Chapter 10: Conclusion: Leading with AI in a Transformative Era

Conclusion: Capitalizing on Artificial Intelligence for Financial Success

The transformative power of artificial intelligence (AI) presents unprecedented opportunities for generating wealth across various sectors. By automating tasks, enhancing decision-making, and creating new business models, AI not only streamlines operations but also opens up new avenues for financial growth. Here, we conclude by summarizing key strategies and considerations for leveraging AI to maximize economic benefits.

Automation and Efficiency

AI significantly boosts productivity by automating routine and complex tasks alike. In industries such as manufacturing, finance, and customer service, AI reduces operational costs and enhances output quality. For instance, AI-powered robots can perform precision tasks faster and with fewer errors than humans. In finance, AI algorithms can manage and analyze large volumes of transactions to detect fraud swiftly, saving millions in potential losses. Businesses that adopt these technologies can redirect their financial resources towards innovation and expansion, thereby driving revenue growth.

Enhanced Decision-Making

AI's ability to analyze vast datasets rapidly enables businesses to make informed decisions quickly. This capability is particularly valuable in dynamic markets where conditions change swiftly. By leveraging predictive analytics, companies can anticipate market trends, adjust strategies in real-time, and stay ahead of competitors. For instance, AI tools in the stock market can analyze patterns to predict stock performance, guiding investors on where to allocate funds to maximize returns.

Personalization at Scale

AI excels in delivering personalized experiences to customers, which is crucial for customer retention and satisfaction. Whether through personalized marketing messages or customized product recommendations, AI's data-driven insights help businesses meet individual customer needs effectively. This level of personalization not only enhances customer engagement but also increases sales. Companies like Amazon and Netflix have successfully used AI to suggest products and movies to users, resulting in higher conversion rates and customer loyalty.

New Market Opportunities

AI opens up new markets and business models that were previously unimaginable. For example, AI-driven health diagnostics tools are making medical consultations more accessible in remote areas, tapping into new customer bases. In the automotive industry, AI is at the forefront of developing self-driving cars, which promises to revolutionize transportation. Entrepreneurs and startups that are quick to explore these emerging fields can gain first-mover advantages and capture significant market share.

Overcoming Barriers with AI

AI also plays a critical role in overcoming barriers to entry in many industries. By reducing the need for large capital investments in areas such as customer research and development, AI levels the playing field for smaller players to compete with established giants. Furthermore, AI-driven platforms can offer services such as real-time translation and business analytics at a fraction of the traditional costs, enabling small businesses to expand globally with reduced language and market entry barriers.

Ethical and Sustainable AI Deployment

While AI offers substantial economic benefits, it is crucial to deploy these technologies ethically and sustainably. Businesses must ensure that their AI systems do not perpetuate biases or infringe on privacy and human rights. Ethical AI practices not only prevent legal and reputational risks but also build trust with consumers and stakeholders, which is invaluable for long-term success.

Moving Forward

For individuals and businesses aiming to harness AI for financial gain, it is essential to stay informed about the latest AI developments and continuously adapt to new technologies. Investing in AI literacy and skills, partnering with AI experts, and experimenting with innovative AI applications are strategic moves that can lead to substantial economic rewards.

In conclusion, AI is not just a technological upgrade but a fundamental shift in how businesses operate and create value. By strategically integrating AI into their operations, companies can not only enhance their current processes but also unlock new opportunities for revenue generation. The era of AI is here, and it holds a wealth of possibilities for those ready to embrace its potential.

www.ingramcontent.com/pod-product-compliance
Lightning Source LLC
LaVergne TN
LVHW081807050326
832903LV00027B/2140